The
Rapture
Manifesto

WHAT TO DO IF YOU ARE LEFT BEHIND

By: Pastor Bill Jenkins

Copyright © 2020
B&B Media
All rights reserved

THE RAPTURE MANIFESTO
WHAT TO DO IF YOU ARE LEFT BEHIND

By Pastor Bill Jenkins

ALL RIGHTS RESERVED
No part of this book may be reproduced, transmitted or copied by any means, electronically or photo duplicated without written permission from the author. Unless otherwise noted, all scripture quotations are from the King James Version of the Bible.

Manufactured in the
United States of America
ISBN # 978-0-578-66881-9

Published by
B&B Media
Upland, CA
Visit the author's website at:
www.pastorbilljenkins.org

Contents

INTRODUCTION 1

CHAPTER 1 5

    What Just Happened?

CHAPTER 2 11

    What Now?

CHAPTER 3 18

    What Next?

CHAPTER 4 32

    What to Do?

CHAPTER 5 37

    What NOT to Do?

CHAPTER 6 42

    What is to Come?

CHAPTER 7 48

    Survival Scriptures

CONCLUSION 56

    The Countdown 59

INTRODUCTION

If millions of people have suddenly disappeared in an instant, without any trace, this book is for you. Please read on! QUICKLY!! The true Christians are gone and will not return for seven years or approximately 2,520 days until Jesus returns with them to establish His kingdom on earth. This book is your manifesto to maneuver through the next 84 months of your life. There is still hope for you to be saved, but you must follow these rules after the Rapture, if you have any chance at spiritual survival. A manifesto is a written statement that describes the strategies and policies that need to be implemented in order to reach an intended goal. The Bible clearly predicts a moment where every follower of Jesus Christ will be "snatched" away to meet with the Lord in the air. Although this was a fantastic event for us as true believers, it is understandable that there is great panic and fear on the earth. Planes have crashed, car wrecks are in abundance, trains have run off the tracks, and chaos is the word of the day. Doctors, nurses, lawyers, judges, factory workers, construction crews, teachers, waiters, waitresses, and store employees have all disappeared. Your friends, family, co-workers, and neighbors are mysteriously gone.

There is no gas or electricity in your houses. All the roadways are crowded, and it is hard to get anywhere. The media is trying to explain away the disappearance of millions of people around the world. Rest assured aliens have not landed in spaceships and finally decided to take us away. This is also not a Marvel movie where Thanos has snapped his fingers and caused us to suddenly evaporate. This is real, and you must act fast because things will only get worse. The reason believers have been removed is to pave the way for some terrible judgments on earth – this is something you need to prepare for, and this book is here to help you. You may already know what is really going on because you have some familiarity with the Bible. Just as the Word declares and we have tried to warn many of you, The Rapture has happened to those of us who accepted Jesus as Savior. We were caught up to be with Him in the air according to 1 Thessalonians 4:13-18. For over 2000 years, the Bible and Christians have been proclaiming to the world that Jesus would be coming back. Jesus stated in John 14:3, "I will come back."

Well ... that day has arrived. The right question to ask is not "why was I left behind?" but "what do I do now that I have been left behind?" That's why I have written this book for you to have a GPS to guide you through some extremely difficult times that are sure to lay ahead. What I am going to tell you is not easy to do but because you rebelled against the truth and rejected God's continuous offers of salvation this is your only way to be saved. You unfortunately have chosen a tough path, and you have no one to blame but yourself. If you are really serious, this time, to serve the Lord you are going to face severe tribulation.

Right now, most of you have three things going through your head:

1. You may think of killing yourself and your family because you are so distraught, mad, and discouraged over what you know has really happened. This will not be the answer to fix the fact that you missed the Rapture. It will only make things worse because some suicide-pact or murder-suicide will not allow for you to escape eternal judgement. You will end up in hell forever.

2. In the coming days, as the Anti-Christ rises to calm the chaos, you will be tempted to make it easy on yourself by not running but instead following the Anti-Christ's instructions. You will be required to receive the Mark of the Beast in some form on your right hand or forehead. This is also something you must not do because it will not fix anything. This

will only make things worse because you will have sided with the devil and will be doomed to eternal judgement. You will end up in hell forever.

3. Your third option, which is definitely not the easiest option, is to take this book and follow the instructions to have a chance at future salvation. You are going to be on the run and be a fugitive of the new law of the Anti-Christ for the next seven years. Honestly, even if you accept this approach most of you will not make it and will quit because this is such a difficult journey, but it is really the only choice you have. Just do it, and do not look back. Read this book, and follow the instructions in order to be saved.

CHAPTER 1
What Just Happened?

What just happened? The Rapture. The actual word "rapture" does not appear in the Bible, however, Paul writes in 1 Thessalonians 4:15-17, *"For this we say unto you by the word of the Lord, that we which are alive and remain unto the coming of the Lord shall not prevent them which are asleep. For the Lord himself shall descend from heaven with a shout, with the voice of the archangel, and with the trump of God: and the dead in Christ shall rise first: Then we which are alive and remain shall be caught up together with them in the clouds, to meet the Lord in the air: and so shall we ever be with the Lord."*

The Greek word for "caught up" in verse 16 is "harpaza" which suggests a rapture of the saints, or catching up of both living and dead, where we will meet the Lord in the air and be taken to heaven to avoid the seven-year Tribulation period.

> *"Watch ye therefore, and pray always, that ye may be accounted worthy to escape all these things that shall come to pass, and to stand before the Son of man." Luke 21:36*

The Rapture is a great event for those who have faithfully served the Lord, but a super scary event for those who rejected or neglected a relationship with Jesus and are now left behind. The Rapture is a doctrine, or a belief presented in the Bible, that has been prophesied to happen for thousands of years. Many of you have heard about this day but have rejected the truth. Some of you even went to church and believed lies and are now going to have to suffer through the Tribulation in order for you to have a chance to make it to heaven. You were warned about this day for years but because of your desire to please yourself, you rejected God and ignored the visual evidence around you that Jesus was coming soon.

Signs of the End Times
(that you obviously ignored)

1. Wars and Rumors of War

   "And ye shall hear of wars and rumours of wars: see that ye be not troubled: for all these things must come to pass, but the end is not yet." Matthew 24:6

2. Famines and Pestilences

   "For nation shall rise against nation, and kingdom against kingdom: and there shall be famines, and pestilences, and earthquakes, in divers places." Matthew 24:7

3. Earthquakes in Strange Places

   "For nation shall rise against nation, and kingdom against kingdom: and there shall be famines, and pestilences, and earthquakes, in divers places." Matthew 24:7

4. Extreme Materialism

   "This know also, that in the last days perilous times shall come. For men shall be lovers of their own selves, covetous, boasters, proud, blasphemers, disobedient to parents, unthankful, unholy," 2 Timothy 3:1-2

5. Disobedient Children

   "For men shall be lovers of their own selves, covetous, boasters, proud, blasphemers, disobedient to parents, unthankful, unholy," 2 Timothy 3:2

6. Universal Substance Abuse

   "Wine is a mocker, strong drink is raging: and whosoever is deceived thereby is not wise." Proverbs 20:1

7. Abnormal Sexual Activity

   "Wherefore God also gave them up to uncleanness through the lusts of their own hearts, to dishonour their own bodies between themselves:....
   26 For this cause God gave them up unto vile affections: for even their women did change the natural use into that which is against nature:
   27 And likewise also the men, leaving the natural use of the woman, burned in their lust one toward another; men with men working that which is unseemly, and receiving in themselves that recompence of their error which was meet....
   29 Being filled with all unrighteousness, fornication, wickedness, covetousness, maliciousness; full of envy, murder, debate, deceit, malignity; whisperers," Romans 1:24-29

8. Slaughter of Innocent Babies

   "Without natural affection, trucebreakers, false accusers, incontinent, fierce, despisers of those that are good," 2 Timothy 3:3

9. Great Disunity and Violence

   "Neither repented they of their murders, nor of their sorceries, nor of their fornication, nor of their thefts." Revelation 9:21

10. People who Commit Evil and Not Feel Guilt

    "Speaking lies in hypocrisy; having their conscience seared with a hot iron;" 1 Timothy 4:2

11. Rejection of God's Word

    "For the time will come when they will not endure sound doctrine; but after their own lusts shall they heap to themselves teachers, having itching ears; And they shall turn away their ears from the truth, and shall be turned unto fables." 2 Timothy 4:3-4

Those were a few of the signs that you missed or ignored. I know you are beating yourself up because you missed these obvious signs. This is not a time to look back, it is a time to move forward.

There were probably a few things you may have noticed when people started to vanish:

1. A loud shout
2. A voice that spoke something you may not have understood
3. A sound of a trumpet
4. Sights or shadows of people ascending into the heavens

Once the initial shock wears off that people are missing, you will begin to hear the news media report that graves all over the world have opened and the bodies are gone. I tell this to you, so you know this is not an alien invasion or a Hollywood movie. There is only one explanation. The Rapture has taken place, millions are missing, and you have been left behind.

CHAPTER 2

What Now?

Right now, you need to come to terms with the fact that Jesus has returned to gather millions of dedicated followers, and you were not one of them. Whether you were marginally serving the Lord by going to church as a duty, or a total reprobate, the fact you are reading this book after the Rapture is a sign you missed out on the greatest event in history. However, there is still hope!

I know you are scared and devastated. You are probably embarrassed because you are still around and looking for others who are gone or remain on earth. However, there is no time to waste. Here are a few things you must immediately do:

1. Get all your money out of the bank. Use it fast to buy what you need; it will soon become worthless.

2. Go to the store and gather band-aids, gauze, rubbing alcohol, sunscreen lotion, and as much over-the-counter pain medication that is available.

3. Buy non-perishable food items. You will need them before you must start living off the land.

4. Get a full tank of gas in all vehicles; it might be your last.

5. Make sure your car has blankets and a few warm clothes for all your family members.

6. You will need a gun or at least a few sharp knives.

7. Matches, matches, and more matches!

8. Grab a Bible.

9. Get out of the large cities, and go to the country; be ready to hide in the hills.

10. Transistor radio and tons of batteries.

I will give you more instructions in the coming chapters, but for now that will be a good start. Obviously, you should do nothing until you pray. And since it was not important to you before now, here is a great sinners prayer to pray to make your heart right with God.

> *Dear Lord Jesus, I am sorry for my sins. I am sorry for not making my life right with You before now. But I ask You to please forgive me of my sins and cleanse me from all unrighteousness. I am a rebellious sinner who refused to accept You before today, but now I know how wrong I am. Forgive me of my sins and wash me in Your blood. Give me strength and determination to make it through these next seven years of tribulation. In Jesus name I pray, Amen.*

There is tons of craziness going on right now, so prepare yourself for a man to rise up to offer a solution to the world to bring peace in the midst of confusion. This is the Anti-Christ or the False Christ that some will accept as the Messiah. Here are a few Biblical characteristics of the Anti-Christ to help you to understand how the Bible identifies him:

- He will be strong militarily, politically, financially, and religiously

    "And in the latter time of their kingdom, when the transgressors are come to the full, a king of fierce countenance, and understanding dark sentences, shall stand up. And his power shall be mighty, but not by his

own power: and he shall destroy wonderfully, and shall prosper, and practise, and shall destroy the mighty and the holy people." Daniel 8:23-24

"And I saw, and behold a white horse: and he that sat on him had a bow; and a crown was given unto him: and he went forth conquering, and to conquer." Revelation 6:2

"And all that dwell upon the earth shall worship him, whose names are not written in the book of life of the Lamb slain from the foundation of the world." Revelation 13:8

"And the beast that was, and is not, even he is the eighth, and is of the seven, and goeth into perdition. And the ten horns which thou sawest are ten kings, which have received no kingdom as yet; but receive power as kings one hour with the beast." Revelation 17:11-12

- He will be energized by Satan

"And the beast which I saw was like unto a leopard, and his feet were as the feet of a bear, and his mouth as the mouth of a lion: and the dragon gave him his power, and his seat, and great authority." Revelation 13:2

- He will use deception to prosper

    "And with all deceivableness of unrighteousness in them that perish; because they received not the love of the truth, that they might be saved." 2 Thessalonians 2:10

- He will set himself up as God

    "And the king shall do according to his will; and he shall exalt himself, and magnify himself above every god, and shall speak marvellous things against the God of gods, and shall prosper till the indignation be accomplished: for that that is determined shall be done. Neither shall he regard the God of his fathers, nor the desire of women, nor regard any god: for he shall magnify himself above all." Daniel 11:36-37

- He will move in signs and wonders

    "Even him, whose coming is after the working of Satan with all power and signs and lying wonders," 2 Thessalonians 2:9

- His name will be related to 666 in a non-obvious way

   "And that no man might buy or sell, save he that had the mark, or the name of the beast, or the number of his name. Here is wisdom. Let him that hath understanding count the number of the beast: for it is the number of a man; and his number is Six hundred threescore and six." Revelation 13:17-18

- He will try and change the calendar and announce a New Era

   "And he shall speak great words against the most High, and shall wear out the saints of the most High, and think to change times and laws: and they shall be given into his hand until a time and times and the dividing of time." Daniel 7:25

- He ultimately will be destroyed

   "And the beast was taken, and with him the false prophet that wrought miracles before

him, with which he deceived them that had received the mark of the beast, and them that worshipped his image. These both were cast alive into a lake of fire burning with brimstone." Revelation 19:20

Do not be deceived! The Anti-Christ is not here to help you. He is here to destroy any remnants left of the true Christ. He will want you to become part of the world community of brotherhood by accepting the mark of the beast to unify humankind. Do not do it or your second chance with God is over! The Anti-Christ not only opposes Christ, but will attempt to take His place. He will lie to seduce those remaining to serve him and not the real Christ. Listen, there is no time to waste. Grab your supplies, and do everything I told you. Go! Now!

CHAPTER 3
What Next?

There are three sets of seven judgements that are about to take place over the next seven years. The Bible refers to these three sets as: the Seals, the Trumpets, and the Bowls. There are a total of 21 judgements the earth will face, and you will have to endure, as a result of your rebellion against God and missing the Rapture. A judgement is a verdict or decision that is handed down after all the facts have been presented. A judgement from God is an official ruling from the highest court. It cannot be appealed or changed. It is a divine sentence that is imposed as a result of your actions. If you missed the Rapture, your actions have been judged as disobedient to God's Word. You have been found GUILTY! All of these judgments will be levied against you. Hold on! These will not be easy to read and hear.

The Seven Seals
Revelation 6:1 – 8:1

Seal #1 - The Anti-Christ will be revealed to lead the world.

"And I saw, and behold a white horse: and he that sat on him had a bow; and a crown was given unto him: and he went forth conquering, and to conquer." Revelation 6:2

Seal #2 - There will be wars among the nations as countries place blame on the disappearance of millions.

"And when he had opened the second seal, I heard the second beast say, Come and see. And there went out another horse that was red: and power was given to him that sat thereon to take peace from the earth, and that they should kill one another: and there was given unto him a great sword." Revelation 6:3-4

Seal #3 - There will be a famine in the land with no food left on store shelves.

"And when he had opened the third seal, I heard the third beast say, Come and see. And I beheld, and lo a black horse; and he that sat on him had a pair of balances in his hand. And I heard a voice in the midst of the four beasts say, A measure of wheat for a penny,

and three measures of barley for a penny; and see thou hurt not the oil and the wine." Revelation 6:5-6

Seal #4 - There will be massive murder in the streets as people attempt to rob others to provide for themselves. This will also include mass suicides.

"And when he had opened the fourth seal, I heard the voice of the fourth beast say, Come and see. And I looked, and behold a pale horse: and his name that sat on him was Death, and Hell followed with him. And power was given unto them over the fourth part of the earth, to kill with sword, and with hunger, and with death, and with the beasts of the earth." Revelation 6:7-8

Seal #5 - There will be an attempt to find people who went to church but didn't make the Rapture. They will try to make them martyrs.

"And when he had opened the fifth seal, I saw under the altar the souls of them that were slain for the word of God, and for the testimony which they held: And they cried

with a loud voice, saying, How long, O Lord, holy and true, dost thou not judge and avenge our blood on them that dwell on the earth? And white robes were given unto every one of them; and it was said unto them, that they should rest yet for a little season, until their fellowservants also and their brethren, that should be killed as they were, should be fulfilled." Revelation 6:9-11

Seal #6 - There will be severe earthquakes and natural disasters that will invade the land.

"And I beheld when he had opened the sixth seal, and, lo, there was a great earthquake; and the sun became black as sackcloth of hair, and the moon became as blood; And the stars of heaven fell unto the earth, even as a fig tree casteth her untimely figs, when she is shaken of a mighty wind." Revelation 6:12-13

Seal #7 - There will be a moment of silence of a half an hour to prepare you for the next set of judgements.

"And when he had opened the seventh seal, there was silence in heaven about the space of half an hour." Revelation 8:1

The Seven Trumpets
Revelation 8 – 11

Trumpet #1 - Hail, fire, and blood will rain down on earth and destroy at least one-third of all plant life and vegetation.

"The first angel sounded, and there followed hail and fire mingled with blood, and they were cast upon the earth: and the third part of trees was burnt up, and all green grass was burnt up." Revelation 8:7

Trumpet #2 - A burning mountain will fall into the oceans, and the waters will turn to blood and kill one-third of all sea life.

"And the second angel sounded, and as it were a great mountain burning with fire was cast into the sea: and the third part of the sea became blood; And the third part of the creatures which were in the sea, and had life,

died; and the third part of the ships were destroyed." Revelation 8:8-9

Trumpet #3 - A star will fall from Heaven called Wormwood (Bitter) and will poison one-third of all the fresh water.

"And the third angel sounded, and there fell a great star from heaven, burning as it were a lamp, and it fell upon the third part of the rivers, and upon the fountains of waters; And the name of the star is called Wormwood: and the third part of the waters became wormwood; and many men died of the waters, because they were made bitter." Revelation 8:10-11

Trumpet #4 - Darkness will cover one-third of the earth.

"And the fourth angel sounded, and the third part of the sun was smitten, and the third part of the moon, and the third part of the stars; so as the third part of them was darkened, and the day shone not for a third part of it, and the night likewise." Revelation 8:12

Trumpet #5 - Demon locusts with human faces, long hair, lions teeth, and the sting of a scorpion will bite people on the earth for five months. It will hurt so badly you will wish you were dead.

"And the shapes of the locusts were like unto horses prepared unto battle; and on their heads were as it were crowns like gold, and their faces were as the faces of men. And they had hair as the hair of women, and their teeth were as the teeth of lions. And they had breastplates, as it were breastplates of iron; and the sound of their wings was as the sound of chariots of many horses running to battle. And they had tails like unto scorpions, and there were stings in their tails: and their power was to hurt men five months." Revelation 9:7-10

Trumpet #6 - Four demons are released with fire and sulfur in their mouths to kill one-third of mankind.

"And the sixth angel sounded, and I heard a voice from the four horns of the golden altar which is before God, Saying to the sixth angel which had the trumpet, Loose the four angels

which are bound in the great river Euphrates. And the four angels were loosed, which were prepared for an hour, and a day, and a month, and a year, for to slay the third part of men. And the number of the army of the horsemen were two hundred thousand thousand: and I heard the number of them. And thus I saw the horses in the vision, and them that sat on them, having breastplates of fire, and of jacinth, and brimstone: and the heads of the horses were as the heads of lions; and out of their mouths issued fire and smoke and brimstone. By these three was the third part of men killed, by the fire, and by the smoke, and by the brimstone, which issued out of their mouths." Revelation 9:13-18

Trumpet #7 - There is another short break where the heavens open to reveal the Presence of God and give a glimpse of Heaven. This might be the worst judgement in that you get to see what you missed out on by not being right with God and missing out on the Rapture.

"And the seventh angel sounded; and there were great voices in heaven, saying, The kingdoms of this world are become the kingdoms of our Lord, and of his Christ; and he shall reign for ever and ever. And the four and twenty elders, which sat before God on their seats, fell upon their faces, and worshipped God, Saying, We give thee thanks, O Lord God Almighty, which art, and wast, and art to come; because thou hast taken to thee thy great power, and hast reigned. And the nations were angry, and thy wrath is come, and the time of the dead, that they should be judged, and that thou shouldest give reward unto thy servants the prophets, and to the saints, and them that fear thy name, small and great; and shouldest destroy them which destroy the earth. And the temple of God was opened in heaven, and there was seen in his temple the ark of his testament: and there were lightnings, and voices, and thunderings, and an earthquake, and great hail." Revelation 11:15-19

The Seven Bowls
Revelation 16

Bowl #1 - Painful sores will come upon those who accepted the Mark of the Beast.

"And the first went, and poured out his vial upon the earth; and there fell a noisome and grievous sore upon the men which had the mark of the beast, and upon them which worshipped his image." Revelation 16:2

Bowl #2 - All living sea creatures that lived through the trumpet judgements will be killed.

"And the second angel poured out his vial upon the sea; and it became as the blood of a dead man: and every living soul died in the sea." Revelation 16:3

Bowl #3 - All waters will turn into blood.

"And the third angel poured out his vial upon the rivers and fountains of waters; and they became blood. And I heard the angel of the

waters say, Thou art righteous, O Lord, which art, and wast, and shalt be, because thou hast judged thus." Revelation 16:4-5

Bowl #4 - Global warming will have a true impact as the sun will intensely burn the skin of people.

"And the fourth angel poured out his vial upon the sun; and power was given unto him to scorch men with fire." Revelation 16:8

Bowl #5 - Darkness will cover the earth and create a panic that will cause people to chew their own tongues.

"And the fifth angel poured out his vial upon the seat of the beast; and his kingdom was full of darkness; and they gnawed their tongues for pain, And blasphemed the God of heaven because of their pains and their sores, and repented not of their deeds." Revelation 16:10-11

Bowl #6 - The Euphrates River will be completely dried up, preparing the way for Jesus and Satan to meet for the final battle called Armageddon.

> *"And the sixth angel poured out his vial upon the great river Euphrates; and the water thereof was dried up, that the way of the kings of the east might be prepared." Revelation 16:12*

Bowl #7 - The worst earthquake of all time will split Jerusalem into three parts. Mountains and islands will disappear, and 100-pound hailstones will fall upon the people as Jesus declares victory over the enemy.

> *"And the seventh angel poured out his vial into the air; and there came a great voice out of the temple of heaven, from the throne, saying, It is done. And there were voices, and thunders, and lightnings; and there was a great earthquake, such as was not since men were upon the earth, so mighty an earthquake, and so great. And the great city was divided into three parts, and the cities of the nations fell: and great Babylon came in*

remembrance before God, to give unto her the cup of the wine of the fierceness of his wrath. And every island fled away, and the mountains were not found. And there fell upon men a great hail out of heaven, every stone about the weight of a talent: and men blasphemed God because of the plague of the hail; for the plague thereof was exceeding great." Revelation 16:17-21

That was a lot there to digest. There will be many things you will have to go through to make it to the reunion party with Jesus and those who were raptured. You will have to make it through unbelievable historical events in order to be saved. It could have been different, but the reality is, you chose this path. To sum up what is next, here is a few helpful hints:

1. Pray to God for strength.

2. Endure without giving into the massive destruction going on around you.

3. Refuse to accept the Mark of the Beast.

4. Do whatever is necessary to protect yourself and your family during this time of war.

5. Never blame God for what you created.

It is not going to be easy, but it is not impossible. You can do this with the help of Jesus.

> *"But Jesus beheld them, and said unto them, With men this is impossible; but with God all things are possible." Matthew 19:26*

CHAPTER 4

What to Do?

This is a simple "to-do-list". I am not here to waste your time, but give you simple, practical things you need to do to make it through this rough seven-year Tribulation period.

To-Do-List

1. Pray

   "Be careful for nothing; but in every thing by prayer and supplication with thanksgiving let your requests be made known unto God." Philippians 4:6

2. Read Psalms

   The Psalms are songs that David and others wrote during difficult times of tribulation.

   ### Psalms 23

   "The Lord is my shepherd; I shall not want.

2 He maketh me to lie down in green pastures: he leadeth me beside the still waters.

3 He restoreth my soul: he leadeth me in the paths of righteousness for his name's sake.

4 Yea, though I walk through the valley of the shadow of death, I will fear no evil: for thou art with me; thy rod and thy staff they comfort me.

5 Thou preparest a table before me in the presence of mine enemies: thou anointest my head with oil; my cup runneth over.

6 Surely goodness and mercy shall follow me all the days of my life: and I will dwell in the house of the Lord for ever."

3. Gather your supplies and leave home

   Don't stay in your homes because it will only be a matter of time before they find you.

4. Drive to a rural or mountainous location to ditch the car, and walk several miles before stopping to rest

Moving on a continual basis, even short distances, is a key to survival. Try to stay close to some source of water that has life in it.

5. Protect yourself and family at all costs from being captured by the forces of the Anti-Christ

   If you have to kill someone, you do what you must do to protect yourself and your loved ones. Although murder is a sin, self-defense is not a crime. God will support you defending your family against evil invasions.

6. Pray for the peace of Jerusalem

   The Jewish people will be under great pressure to accept the Anti-Christ as the Messiah.

   "Pray for the peace of Jerusalem:" Psalm 122:6a

7. Mark the days

    The Tribulation will last approximately 2520 days, so have a goal to make it through all of them. I have put a calendar in the back of this book for you to literally mark the days.

8. Be prepared to suffer

    This is going to be a tough journey. Accept it.

9. Be prepared to eat things you never thought you would eat

    If you are hungry, you will eat just about anything. You will have to live off the land to survive.

10. Be determined to endure

    "If we suffer, we shall also reign with him: if we deny him, he also will deny us:" 2 Timothy 2:12

I am sure there are more things that could be added. As you continue this journey, you will no doubt be able to add to this list. Be strong and of good courage.

Do not give up!!

CHAPTER 5

What NOT to Do?

Just as there are things you should be doing, there are also things you should not be doing during this seven-year time of tribulation. Take all these things seriously, and do not let your guard down, or it could lead to you being caught by the military force of the Anti-Christ. If you do not submit to the new laws of the New World Order, you will be a fugitive and considered a criminal. It is important to run and hide to avoid capture. If for some reason you are captured, you will be given a choice to accept the Mark of the Beast or be beheaded.

> *"And I saw thrones, and they sat upon them, and judgment was given unto them: and I saw the souls of them that were beheaded for the witness of Jesus, and for the word of God, and which had not worshipped the beast, neither his image, neither had received his mark upon their foreheads, or in their hands; and they lived and reigned with Christ a thousand years." Revelation 20:4*

Do Not Do List

1. Do not go to church

   This is hard for a pastor to say, but avoid church buildings. It will be the first place the soldiers of the Anti-Christ will look for you.

2. Do not keep your cell phone

   Your cell phone can be tracked, so do not take the chance of being found by keeping it. This is going to be hard to do because most people have an addiction to their phones. Do not try and compromise. You must get rid of your phone, if you are going to survive.

3. Do not commit suicide

   This will probably run through your mind, but do not do it. It will not solve your problem, and it is not an escape to get to heaven. Suicide is self-murder, and it will not gain you freedom from tribulation and entrance into the pearly gates.

4. Do not gather or stay in groups of more than 15 people

   It is important to limit the amount of people in your group if you are traveling together. Jesus and the Disciples made 13 people, so monitor and limit the people in your group. Make sure those you are with are as serious about serving the Lord and making it through the Tribulation as you are.

5. Do not get rid of silver or gold

   Any silver or gold needs to be kept as a commodity that could be used to trade for other necessary items with other travelers trying to make it through the Tribulation. Gold or silver coins or jewelry must be kept and protected for your valuable use in the future days ahead.

6. Do not believe any other explanation for the massive disappearances other than it is because of the Rapture

   I promise you the media will do their best to explain away what has happened. Do not believe them.

7. Do not accept the Mark of the Beast

   Under NO circumstances are you to accept the Mark of the Beast. They may attempt to torture you or worse, torture your spouse and children, to get you to cave in and accept the Mark of the Beast. Do not give in, or you are out of strikes and the game is over.

8. Do not take what you cannot carry

   Be smart about what you take with you. Limit your load.

9. Do not use credit cards

   Credit card transactions can be traced and lead to your capture and eventually torture.

10. Do not have babies

    This is no time to bring a baby into this world.

11. Do not give up

    This is the best piece of advice I can give. Do not give up! Be a warrior for Jesus!!

You must take this list seriously. Do not talk yourself into doing anything you should not do. You will be tempted to not fully follow these instructions. However, I promise if you do not obey, you will be caught and captured. Do not pick and choose what you want to follow. Listen to every word in order to survive.

CHAPTER 6

What is to Come?

This could be the most hopeful chapter in this book because the Battle of Armageddon marks the end of the Tribulation period. If you make it to this point, you are probably good for eternity. You will also have a great appreciation for what salvation really means. The Battle of Armageddon is the final battle between good and evil. It is the ultimate fight of all-time between Jesus and the Devil. Israel will be at the center of the conflict with at least six major powers involved against them to destroy them. The new Roman Empire, Russia, Asia, and Africa, among others, will assemble as a United Nations military force to destroy Israel. The Bible tells us that when the nations are gathered against Jerusalem, that the Army of the Lord will return. The angels and those who were raptured seven years earlier, along with the Old and New Testament saints, will join with those on earth who made it through the Tribulation to watch Jesus destroy the Devil and all the power of the Anti-Christ.

"His eyes were as a flame of fire, and on his head were many crowns; and he had a name written, that no man knew, but he himself.

13 And he was clothed with a vesture dipped in blood: and his name is called The Word of God.

14 And the armies which were in heaven followed him upon white horses, clothed in fine linen, white and clean.

15 And out of his mouth goeth a sharp sword, that with it he should smite the nations: and he shall rule them with a rod of iron: and he treadeth the winepress of the fierceness and wrath of Almighty God.

16 And he hath on his vesture and on his thigh a name written, King Of Kings, And Lord Of Lords." Revelation 19:12-16

He will slay the enemy with the sword as we watch and cheer on our Savior and Lord. Jesus will throw the Anti-Christ, the False Prophet, and Satan himself into a lake of fire and the Battle of Armageddon will be over. Jesus and His followers will declare VICTORY!

Here will be some of the final results:

1. Blood will spread over a 200-mile area, and the blood will be as high as four feet deep.

   "And the winepress was trodden without the city, and blood came out of the winepress, even unto the horse bridles, by the space of a thousand and six hundred furlongs." Revelation 14:20

2. The birds of the air will eat the flesh of the dead bodies in the battlefield.

   "And the remnant were slain with the sword of him that sat upon the horse, which sword proceeded out of his mouth: and all the fowls were filled with their flesh." Revelation 19:21

3. It will take seven months to bury the dead and seven years to get rid of all the natural weapons used during the battle.

   "And they that dwell in the cities of Israel shall go forth, and shall set on fire and burn the weapons, both the shields and the bucklers, the bows and the arrows, and the

handstaves, and the spears, and they shall burn them with fire seven years.

And seven months shall the house of Israel be burying of them, that they may cleanse the land." Ezekiel 39:9 &12

4. The Millennial period will begin when Jesus and His Saints will rule the earth for 1,000 years.

   "And I saw thrones, and they sat upon them, and judgment was given unto them: and I saw the souls of them that were beheaded for the witness of Jesus, and for the word of God, and which had not worshipped the beast, neither his image, neither had received his mark upon their foreheads, or in their hands; and they lived and reigned with Christ a thousand years. But the rest of the dead lived not again until the thousand years were finished. This is the first resurrection." Revelation 20:4-5

5. During this Millennial period, there will not be murders, thefts, or crimes. Even the animals will not kill one another as they too will eat of foods produced from seeds.

"There shall be no more thence an infant of days, nor an old man that hath not filled his days: for the child shall die an hundred years old; but the sinner being an hundred years old shall be accursed.

21 And they shall build houses, and inhabit them; and they shall plant vineyards, and eat the fruit of them.

22 They shall not build, and another inhabit; they shall not plant, and another eat: for as the days of a tree are the days of my people, and mine elect shall long enjoy the work of their hands.

23 They shall not labour in vain, nor bring forth for trouble; for they are the seed of the blessed of the Lord, and their offspring with them.

24 And it shall come to pass, that before they call, I will answer; and while they are yet speaking, I will hear.

25 The wolf and the lamb shall feed together, and the lion shall eat straw like the bullock: and dust shall be the serpent's meat. They shall not hurt nor destroy in all my holy mountain, saith the Lord." Isaiah 65:20-25

I am going to stop there, although there is more to come. Let us get to the Battle of Armageddon first, which will be quite the task.

CHAPTER 7
Survival Scriptures

Put on the Armor of God daily

"Finally, my brethren, be strong in the Lord, and in the power of his might.

11 Put on the whole armour of God, that ye may be able to stand against the wiles of the devil.

12 For we wrestle not against flesh and blood, but against principalities, against powers, against the rulers of the darkness of this world, against spiritual wickedness in high places.

13 Wherefore take unto you the whole armour of God, that ye may be able to withstand in the evil day, and having done all, to stand.

14 Stand therefore, having your loins girt about with truth, and having on the breastplate of righteousness;

15 And your feet shod with the preparation of the gospel of peace

16 Above all, taking the shield of faith, wherewith ye shall be able to quench all the fiery darts of the wicked.

17 And take the helmet of salvation, and the sword of the Spirit, which is the word of God:

18 Praying always with all prayer and supplication in the Spirit, and watching thereunto with all perseverance and supplication for all saints;"
Ephesians 6:10-18

Endure until the End

"But he that shall endure unto the end, the same shall be saved."
Matthew 24:13

Heaven is Our Hope

"And I saw a new heaven and a new earth: for the first heaven and the first earth were passed away; and there was no more sea.

2 And I John saw the holy city, new Jerusalem, coming down from God out of heaven, prepared as a bride adorned for her husband.

3 And I heard a great voice out of heaven saying, Behold, the tabernacle of God is with men, and he will dwell with them, and they shall be his people, and God himself shall be with them, and be their God.

4 And God shall wipe away all tears from their eyes; and there shall be no more death, neither sorrow, nor crying, neither shall there be any more pain: for the former things are passed away.

5 And he that sat upon the throne said, Behold, I make all things new. And he said unto me, Write: for these words are true and faithful.

6 And he said unto me, It is done. I am Alpha and Omega, the beginning and the end. I will give unto him that is athirst of the fountain of the water of life freely." Revelation 21:1-6

All Scripture is Good

> *"All scripture is given by inspiration of God, and is profitable for doctrine, for reproof, for correction, for instruction in righteousness: That the man of God may be perfect, thoroughly furnished unto all good works."*
> *2 Timothy 3:16-17*

Bear the Fruit of the Spirit

> *"But the fruit of the Spirit is love, joy, peace, longsuffering, gentleness, goodness, faith, Meekness, temperance: against such there is no law." Galatians 5:22-23*

God Loves You

> *"For God so loved the world, that he gave his only begotten Son, that whosoever believeth in him should not perish, but have everlasting life."*
> *John 3:16*

God Gives Grace

"Thus saith the Lord, The people which were left of the sword found grace in the wilderness; even Israel, when I went to cause him to rest."
Jeremiah 31:2

Fear God, Not Man

"And fear not them which kill the body, but are not able to kill the soul: but rather fear him which is able to destroy both soul and body in hell."
Matthew 10:28

The Lord Will Answer When You Call

"Call unto me, and I will answer thee, and show thee great and mighty things, which thou knowest not."
Jeremiah 33:3

Survival Instructions

"Rejoicing in hope; patient in tribulation; continuing instant in prayer;" Romans 12:12

Christ is Your Strength

"I can do all things through Christ which strengtheneth me." Philippians 4:13

Crucified with Christ

"I am crucified with Christ: nevertheless I live; yet not I, but Christ liveth in me: and the life which I now live in the flesh I live by the faith of the Son of God, who loved me, and gave himself for me." Galatians 2:20

Do Not Fear

"For God hath not given us the spirit of fear; but of power, and of love, and of a sound mind." 2 Timothy 1:7

Love

"Charity suffereth long, and is kind; charity envieth not; charity vaunteth not itself, is not puffed up,

5 Doth not behave itself unseemly, seeketh not her own, is not easily provoked, thinketh no evil;

6 Rejoiceth not in iniquity, but rejoiceth in the truth;

7 Beareth all things, believeth all things, hopeth all things, endureth all things.

8 Charity never faileth: but whether there be prophecies, they shall fail; whether there be tongues, they shall cease; whether there be knowledge, it shall vanish away."
1 Corinthians 13:4-8

God Works Everything Out for Our Good

"And we know that all things work together for good to them that love God, to them who are the called according to his purpose."
Romans 8:28

God is With You

> *"Fear thou not; for I am with thee: be not dismayed; for I am thy God: I will strengthen thee; yea, I will help thee; yea, I will uphold thee with the right hand of my righteousness." Isaiah 41:10*

CONCLUSION

This is not a book for the righteous but for those who missed the Rapture. This is your survival guide for the Tribulation. For what it is worth, I literally hand wrote this entire book in one day. It was about an eight-hour period where I felt totally compelled and anointed to give you these words for such a time as this. I wish there was a better way, but this the only way you can be saved since you rejected the Lord before the Rapture.

When I was a young teenager, the Lord gave me a dream at the altar. The dream was so real about what was to happen in my life that it scared me to the point I backslid and ran away from the Lord. One part of the dream was that I would write a survivors guide for those who missed the Rapture. Well, 40 years later… here it is. The words of this book were divinely given by God to me as I wrote for about eight hours straight.

This book is designed to help you and provide a second chance at salvation. **DO NOT BLOW IT!** I totally feel these are words from God and not my own. If you have been left behind, I know you are scared and embarrassed, but there is still hope although you missed the Rapture. Repent of your sins, and be willing to endure unto the end.

In case you did not take the time to say the sinners prayer earlier, I want to give you another chance to do it now.

> *Dear Lord Jesus, I am sorry for my sins. I am sorry for not making my life right with You before now. But I ask You to please forgive me of my sins and cleanse me from all unrighteousness. I am a rebellious sinner who refused to accept You before today, but now I know how wrong I am. Forgive me of my sins and wash me in Your blood. Give me strength and determination to make it through these next seven years of tribulation. In Jesus name I pray, Amen.*

There is one more crucial thing for you to remember. It is a divine scripture for those of you fighting to make it through the Tribulation.

> *"And they overcame him by the blood of the Lamb, and by the word of their testimony; and they loved not their lives unto the death." Revelation 12:11*

It will take all three of these things to survive:

1. Blood of Jesus

Spiritually pray to cover yourself in the blood of Jesus. You are obviously not putting blood on yourself but applying the shed blood of Jesus Christ to your everyday life as a shield of protection.

2. The word of your testimony

   Your testimony is that you missed the Rapture, but you are trying to prove that you learned a lesson and fight for your salvation. Fight with your words and be positive with what comes out of your mouth.

3. Be willing to give your life

   It might seriously cost you your life on earth to find true life with Christ for Eternity.

The Great Tribulation is here, so be brave.

GODSPEED

The Countdown
Start counting the days on the day after the Rapture.

1 2 3 4 5 6 7 8 9 10 11 12 13 14 15 16 17 18 19 20
21 22 23 24 25 26 27 28 29 30 31 32 33 34 35 36 37
38 39 40 41 42 43 44 45 46 47 48 49 50 51 52 53 54
55 56 57 58 59 60 61 62 63 64 65 66 67 68 69 70 71
72 73 74 75 76 77 78 79 80 81 82 83 84 85 86 87 88
89 90 91 92 93 94 95 96 97 98 99 100 101 102 103
104 105 106 107 108 109 110 111 112 113 114 115
116 117 118 119 120 121 122 123 124 125 126 127
128 129 130 131 132 133 134 135 136 137 138 139
140 141 142 143 144 145 146 147 148 149 150 151
152 153 154 155 156 157 158 159 160 161 162 163
164 165 166 167 168 169 170 171 172 173 174 175
176 177 178 179 180 181 182 183 184 185 186 187
188 189 190 191 192 193 194 195 196 197 198 199
200 201 202 203 204 205 206 207 208 209 210 211
212 213 214 215 216 217 218 219 220 221 222 223
224 225 226 227 228 229 230 231 232 233 234 235
236 237 238 239 240 241 242 243 244 245 246 247
248 249 250 251 252 253 254 255 256 257 258 259
260 261 262 263 264 265 266 267 268 269 270 271
272 273 274 275 276 277 278 279 280 281 282 283
284 285 286 287 288 289 290 291 292 293 294 295
296 297 298 299 300 301 302 303 304 305 306 307
308 309 310 311 312 313 314 315 316 317 318 319
320 321 322 323 324 325 326 327 328 329 330 331
332 333 334 335 336 337 338 339 340 341 342 343
344 345 346 347 348 349 350 351 352 353 354 355

356 357 358 359 360 361 362 363 364 365 366 367
368 369 370 371 372 373 374 375 376 377 378 379
380 381 382 383 384 385 386 387 388 389 390 391
392 393 394 395 396 397 398 399 400 401 402 403
404 405 406 407 408 409 410 411 412 413 414 415
416 417 418 419 420 421 422 423 424 425 426 427
428 429 430 431 432 433 434 435 436 437 438 439
440 441 442 443 444 445 446 447 448 449 450 451
452 453 454 455 456 457 458 459 460 461 462 463
464 465 466 467 468 469 470 471 472 473 474 475
476 477 478 479 480 481 482 483 484 485 486 487
488 489 490 491 492 493 494 495 496 497 498 499
500 501 502 503 504 505 506 507 508 509 510 511
512 513 514 515 516 517 518 519 520 521 522 523
524 525 526 527 528 529 530 531 532 533 534 535
536 537 538 539 540 541 542 543 544 545 546 547
548 549 550 551 552 553 554 555 556 557 558 559
560 561 562 563 564 565 566 567 568 569 570 571
572 573 574 575 576 577 578 579 580 581 582 583
584 585 586 587 588 589 590 591 592 593 594 595
596 597 598 599 600 601 602 603 604 605 606 607
608 609 610 611 612 613 614 615 616 617 618 619
620 621 622 623 624 625 626 627 628 629 630 631
632 633 634 635 636 637 638 639 640 641 642 643
644 645 646 647 648 649 650 651 652 653 654 655
656 657 658 659 660 661 662 663 664 665 666 667
668 669 670 671 672 673 674 675 676 677 678 679
680 681 682 683 684 685 686 687 688 689 690 691
692 693 694 695 696 697 698 699 700 701 702 703
704 705 706 707 708 709 710 711 712 713 714 715
716 717 718 719 720 721 722 723 724 725 726 727

728 729 730 731 732 733 734 735 736 737 738 739
740 741 742 743 744 745 746 747 748 749 750 751
752 753 754 755 756 757 758 759 760 761 762 763
764 765 766 767 768 769 770 771 772 773 774 775
776 777 778 779 780 781 782 783 784 785 786 787
788 789 790 791 792 793 794 795 796 797 798 799
800 801 802 803 804 805 806 807 808 809 810 811
812 813 814 815 816 817 818 819 820 821 822 823
824 825 826 827 828 829 830 831 832 833 834 835
836 837 838 839 840 841 842 843 844 845 846 847
848 849 850 851 852 853 854 855 856 857 858 859
860 861 862 863 864 865 866 867 868 869 870 871
872 873 874 875 876 877 878 879 880 881 882 883
884 885 886 887 888 889 890 891 892 893 894 895
896 897 898 899 900 901 902 903 904 905 906 907
908 909 910 911 912 913 914 915 916 917 918 919
920 921 922 923 924 925 926 927 928 929 930 931
932 933 934 935 936 937 938 939 940 941 942 943
944 945 946 947 948 949 950 951 952 953 954 955
956 957 958 959 960 961 962 963 964 965 966 967
968 969 970 971 972 973 974 975 976 977 978 979
980 981 982 983 984 985 986 987 988 989 990 991
992 993 994 995 996 997 998 999 1000 1001 1002
1003 1004 1005 1006 1007 1008 1009 1010 1011
1012 1013 1014 1015 1016 1017 1018 1019 1020
1021 1022 1023 1024 1025 1026 1027 1028 1029
1030 1031 1032 1033 1034 1035 1036 1037 1038
1039 1040 1041 1042 1043 1044 1045 1046 1047
1048 1049 1050 1051 1052 1053 1054 1055 1056
1057 1058 1059 1060 1061 1062 1063 1064 1065
1066 1067 1068 1069 1070 1071 1072 1073 1074

1075 1076 1077 1078 1079 1080 1081 1082 1083
1084 1085 1086 1087 1088 1089 1090 1091 1092
1093 1094 1095 1096 1097 1098 1099 1100 1101
1102 1103 1104 1105 1106 1107 1108 1109 1110
1111 1112 1113 1114 1115 1116 1117 1118 1119
1120 1121 1122 1123 1124 1125 1126 1127 1228
1229 1230 1231 1232 1233 1234 1235 1236 1237
1238 1239 1240 1241 1242 1243 1244 1245 1246
1247 1248 1249 1250 1251 1252 1253 1254 1255
1256 1257 1258 1259 1260 1261 1262 1263 1264
1265 1266 1267 1268 1269 1270 1271 1272 1273
1274 1275 1276 1277 1278 1279 1280 1281 1282
1283 1284 1285 1286 1287 1288 1289 1290 1291
1292 1293 1294 1295 1296 1297 1298 1299 1300
1301 1302 1303 1304 1305 1306 1307 1308 1309
1310 1311 1312 1313 1314 1315 1316 1317 1318
1319 1320 1321 1322 1323 1324 1325 1326 1327
1328 1329 1330 1331 1332 1333 1334 1335 1336
1337 1338 1339 1340 1341 1342 1343 1344 1345
1346 1347 1348 1349 1350 1351 1352 1353 1354
1355 1356 1357 1358 1359 1360 1361 1362 1363
1364 1365 1366 1367 1368 1369 1370 1371 1372
1373 1374 1375 1376 1377 1378 1379 1380 1381
1382 1383 1384 1385 1386 1387 1388 1389 1390
1391 1392 1393 1394 1395 1396 1397 1398 1399
1400 1401 1402 1403 1404 1405 1406 1407 1408
1409 1410 1411 1412 1413 1414 1415 1416 1417
1418 1419 1420 1421 1422 1423 1424 1425 1426
1427 1428 1429 1430 1431 1432 1433 1434 1435
1436 1437 1438 1439 1440 1441 1442 1443 1444
1445 1446 1447 1448 1449 1450 1451 1452 1453

1454 1455 1456 1457 1458 1459 1460 1461 1462
1463 1464 1465 1466 1467 1468 1469 1470 1471
1472 1473 1474 1475 1476 1477 1478 1479 1480
1481 1482 1483 1484 1485 1486 1487 1488 1489
1490 1491 1492 1493 1494 1495 1496 1497 1498
1499 1500 1501 1502 1503 1504 1505 1506 1507
1508 1509 1510 1511 1512 1513 1514 1515 1516
1517 1518 1519 1520 1521 1522 1523 1524 1525
1526 1527 1528 1529 1530 1531 1532 1533 1534
1535 1536 1537 1538 1539 1540 1541 1542 1543
1544 1545 1546 1547 1548 1549 1550 1551 1552
1553 1554 1555 1556 1557 1558 1559 1560 1561
1562 1563 1564 1565 1566 1567 1568 1569 1570
1571 1572 1573 1574 1575 1576 1577 1578 1579
1580 1581 1582 1583 1584 1585 1586 1587 1588
1589 1590 1591 1592 1593 1594 1595 1596 1597
1598 1599 1600 1601 1602 1603 1604 1605 1606
1607 1608 1609 1610 1611 1612 1613 1614 1615
1616 1617 1618 1619 1620 1621 1622 1623 1624
1625 1626 1627 1628 1629 1630 1631 1632 1633
1634 1635 1636 1637 1638 1639 1640 1641 1642
1643 1644 1645 1646 1647 1648 1649 1650 1651
1652 1653 1654 1655 1656 1657 1658 1659 1660
1661 1662 1663 1664 1665 1666 1667 1668 1669
1670 1671 1672 1673 1674 1675 1676 1677 1678
1679 1680 1681 1682 1683 1684 1685 1686 1687
1688 1689 1690 1691 1692 1693 1694 1695 1696
1697 1698 1699 1700 1701 1702 1703 1704 1705
1706 1707 1708 1709 1710 1711 1712 1713 1714
1715 1716 1717 1718 1719 1720 1721 1722 1723
1724 1725 1726 1727 1728 1729 1730 1731 1732

1733 1734 1735 1736 1737 1738 1739 1740 1741
1742 1743 1744 1745 1746 1747 1748 1749 1750
1751 1752 1753 1754 1755 1756 1757 1758 1759
1760 1761 1762 1763 1764 1765 1766 1767 1768
1769 1770 1771 1772 1773 1774 1775 1776 1777
1778 1779 1780 1781 1782 1783 1784 1785 1786
1787 1788 1789 1790 1791 1792 1793 1794 1795
1796 1797 1798 1799 1800 1801 1802 1803 1804
1805 1806 1807 1808 1809 1810 1811 1812 1813
1814 1815 1816 1817 1818 1819 1820 1821 1822
1823 1824 1825 1826 1827 1828 1829 1830 1831
1832 1833 1834 1835 1836 1837 1838 1839 1840
1841 1842 1843 1844 1845 1846 1847 1848 1849
1850 1851 1852 1853 1854 1855 1856 1857 1858
1859 1860 1861 1862 1863 1864 1865 1866 1867
1868 1869 1870 1871 1872 1873 1874 1875 1876
1877 1878 1879 1880 1881 1882 1883 1884 1885
1886 1887 1888 1889 1890 1891 1892 1893 1894
1895 1896 1897 1898 1899 1900 1901 1902 1903
1904 1905 1906 1907 1908 1909 1910 1911 1912
1913 1914 1915 1916 1917 1918 1919 1920 1921
1922 1923 1924 1925 1926 1927 1928 1929 1930
1931 1932 1933 1934 1935 1936 1937 1938 1939
1940 1941 1942 1943 1944 1945 1946 1947 1948
1949 1950 1951 1952 1953 1954 1955 1956 1957
1958 1959 1960 1961 1962 1963 1964 1965 1966
1967 1968 1969 1970 1971 1972 1973 1974 1975
1976 1977 1978 1979 1980 1981 1982 1983 1984
1985 1986 1987 1988 1989 1990 1991 1992 1993
1994 1995 1996 1997 1998 1999 2000 2001 2002
2003 2004 2005 2006 2007 2008 2009 2010 2011

2012 2013 2014 2015 2016 2017 2018 2019 2020
2021 2022 2023 2024 2025 2026 2027 2028 2029
2030 2031 2032 2033 2034 2035 2036 2037 2038
2039 2040 2041 2042 2043 2044 2045 2046 2047
2048 2049 2050 2051 5052 2053 2054 2055 2056
2057 2058 2059 2060 2061 2062 2063 2064 2065
2066 2067 2068 2069 2070 2071 2072 2073 2074
2075 2076 2077 2078 2079 2080 2081 2082 2083
2084 2085 2086 2087 2088 2089 2090 2091 2092
2093 2094 2095 2096 2097 2098 2099 2100 2101
2102 2103 2104 2105 2106 2107 2108 2109 2110
2111 2112 2113 2114 2115 2116 2117 2118 2119
2120 2121 2122 2123 2124 2125 2126 2127 2228
2229 2230 2231 2232 2233 2234 2235 2236 2237
2238 2239 2240 2241 2242 2243 2244 2245 2246
2247 2248 2249 2250 2251 2252 2253 2254 2255
2256 2257 2258 2259 2260 2261 2262 2263 2264
2265 2266 2267 2268 2269 2270 2271 2272 2273
2274 2275 2276 2277 2278 2279 2280 2281 2282
2283 2284 2285 2286 2287 2288 2289 2290 2291
2292 2293 2294 2295 2296 2297 2298 2299 2300
2301 2302 2303 2304 2305 2306 2307 2308 2309
2310 2311 2312 2313 2314 2315 2316 2317 2318
2319 2320 2321 2322 2323 2324 2325 2326 2327
2328 2329 2330 2331 2332 2333 2334 2335 2336
2337 2338 2339 2340 2341 2342 2343 2344 2345
2346 2347 2348 2349 2350 2351 2352 2353 2354
2355 2356 2357 2358 2359 2360 2361 2362 2363
2364 2365 2366 2367 2368 2369 2370 2371 2372
2373 2374 2375 2376 2377 2378 2379 3280 2381
2382 2383 2384 2385 2386 2387 2388 2389 2390

2391 2392 2393 2394 2395 2396 2397 2398 2399
2400 2401 2402 2403 2404 2405 2406 2407 2408
2409 2410 2411 2412 2413 2414 2415 2416 2417
2418 2419 2420 2421 2422 2423 2424 2425 2426
2427 2428 2429 2430 2431 2432 2433 2434 2435
2436 2437 2438 2439 2440 2441 2442 2443 2444
2445 2446 2447 2448 2449 2450 2451 2452 2453
2454 2455 2456 2457 2458 2459 2460 2461 2462
2463 2464 2465 2466 2467 2468 2469 2470 2471
2472 2473 2474 2475 2476 2477 2478 2479 2480
2481 2482 2483 2484 2485 2486 2487 2488 2489
2490 2491 2492 2493 2494 2495 2496 2497 2498
2499 2500 2501 2502 2503 2504 2505 2506 2507
2508 2509 2510 2511 2512 2513 2514 2515 2516
2517 2518 2519 2520

www.ingramcontent.com/pod-product-compliance
Lightning Source LLC
Chambersburg PA
CBHW071842290426
44109CB00017B/1899